WASHINGTON IRVING SCHOOL

Teaneck, N. J.

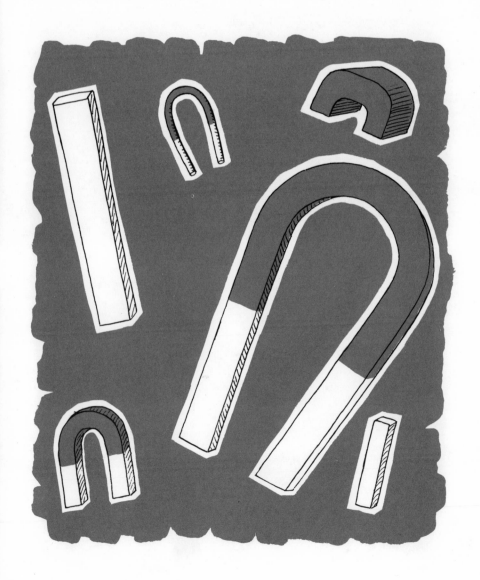

MAGNETS
and how to use them

MAGNETS
and how to use them

TILLIE S. PINE
JOSEPH LEVINE

Illustrated by ANNE MARIE JAUSS

Mc GRAW-HILL BOOK COMPANY
New York   Toronto   London

Also by
Tillie S. Pine and Joseph Levine

THE INDIANS KNEW

THE PILGRIMS KNEW

THE CHINESE KNEW

THE EGYPTIANS KNEW

THE ESKIMOS KNEW

SIMPLE MACHINES AND HOW WE USE THEM

ELECTRICITY AND HOW WE USE IT

AIR ALL AROUND

FRICTION ALL AROUND

GRAVITY ALL AROUND

HEAT ALL AROUND

LIGHT ALL AROUND

SOUNDS ALL AROUND

WATER ALL AROUND

WEATHER ALL AROUND

Library of Congress Catalog Card Number: 58–11187

111213 HDBP 7543210

To Mona and Susan
who always want to know
how *and* why

How do people use magnets in their work?
What things will stick to magnets?
Can a magnet work through things?
What part of the magnet is strongest?
Why do we make horseshoe magnets?
How can magnets be used to help you
    find direction?
What is the right way to use a compass
    that you buy in a store?
How can you make your own magnet?
How can you make
    an on-and-off magnet (electromagnet)?
How can an electromagnet pick up
    and drop a heavy load?
Where do electromagnets work in your home?

This book will show you how to find out!

HOW DO PEOPLE USE MAGNETS IN THEIR WORK?

Tailors use magnets to pick up pins
and needles that have fallen on the floor.

Hairdressers sometimes use magnets
to draw out bobby pins from ladies' hair.

Sign hangers use magnet hammers
to hold the tacks that are used to nail
up signs.

Magnets make work easier!

Teachers sometimes use magnet boards
in school when they teach words and numbers
to children.

People on some television programs
use magnet boards when they play
scrambled word or letter games.

WHAT THINGS WILL STICK TO MAGNETS?

Touch a tack with the end
of your magnet.
What happens?
The tack sticks to the magnet!
Now touch a nail and a clip
and see if they stick to the magnet.
Touch a toothpick, a penny,
a rubber band with the magnet.
What happens now?
They do not stick to the magnet.

Look around in your house and
find a pencil, a book, a bobby pin, a glass,
an eraser, a nail, a pair of scissors, a toy.
Do you think any of these will stick to your
magnet?
Try each one.

If the things you touch have iron
in them, they will stick.

If they do not have iron in them,
they will not stick.

Long magnets
Short magnets
Fat magnets
Thin magnets

Boys and girls play with toys that have magnets in them.

Sailing toys, fishing games, building toys, and trick toys— all have magnets in them.

DANCING GIRL

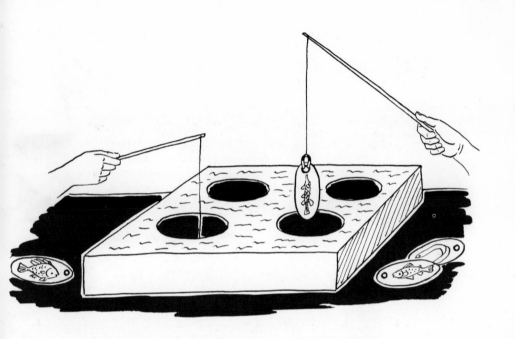

You can have fun playing with
games and toys that have magnets in them.

CAN A MAGNET WORK THROUGH THINGS?

Put a small piece of paper on a table.
Touch the paper with your magnet.
Does it stick?
Of course not!
Why not?
Paper has no iron in it.

Now place the paper over a clip.
Touch the paper right over the clip with your magnet.
Lift!
Up they come—paper, clip, and all!
A magnet, you see, works through paper.

What do you think would happen if you used an open handkerchief instead of paper over the clip?

Exactly the same thing would happen.

A magnet also works through cloth.

Now try this!

Touch a drinking glass with your magnet.

Why doesn't the glass stick to the magnet?

Glass has no iron in it.

Put a clip inside the glass.

Touch the magnet to the outside of the glass near the clip.

Watch the clip move around inside the glass as you slide the magnet around the outside of the glass.

A magnet, you see, works through glass.

Leave the clip in the glass and add water.
Now go fishing for the clip with the magnet.
Surprised?
The clip jumps at the magnet
just as soon as the magnet gets
close to it.
A magnet, you see, works through water.

Magnets make iron things stick
to them.
And—
magnets can work through

paper

cloth

glass

and water!

WHAT PART OF THE MAGNET IS STRONGEST?

You have been using only the ends of the magnet.

Do you think the middle of the magnet can pick up things that have iron in them, just as the ends do?

Try it and see!

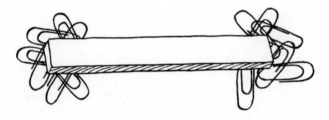

Spread out a few clips on a table.

Lay the magnet on the clips.

Lift!

Up come many clips!

Can you believe what you see?

Clips are sticking only near the ends of the magnet.

And—

there are no clips sticking to the middle of the magnet.

Why not?

Your magnet is strong enough
only at its ends to pick up the clips.

Remember all the things in your
house that you picked up with your magnet?

Now try to pick up these same things
using the middle of your magnet.

You will see that the middle
of your magnet is not strong enough
to pick up these things—only the
ends can do that.

All magnets are strongest
at their ends!

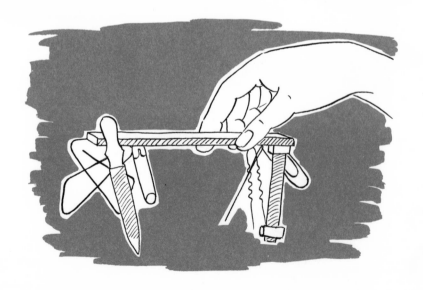

Straight magnets!
Curved magnets!

Both kinds have strong ends!

The ends of magnets are sometimes
far apart like this:

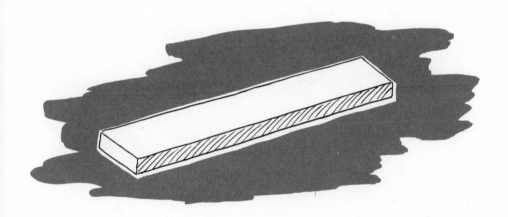

We call this a bar magnet.
We might also call it a stick magnet,
a narrow magnet, or a long magnet.
But we call it a bar magnet.
Everyone calls it a bar magnet.

The ends of a magnet are sometimes close together like this:

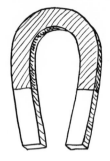

Or like this: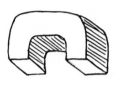

Do you see why we call one
a horseshoe magnet and the other
a U magnet?
We might call these bent magnets,
curved magnets, or fat magnets.
But!
we call them horseshoe magnets
and U magnets.
Everyone calls them horseshoe
magnets and U magnets!

Bar magnets have strong ends
far apart.
Horseshoe magnets and U magnets
have strong ends close together.

WHY DO WE MAKE HORSESHOE MAGNETS AND U MAGNETS?

You can find out why
we make horseshoe magnets and U magnets
by making believe *you* are a magnet.
Spread your arms.
You are a bar magnet.
Your hands are the ends.
Now pick up a chair with one of your
outstretched hands.
Hard, isn't it?

Now try it this way.
Put your hands close together in front of you.
You are a horseshoe magnet or a U magnet.
Your hands are the ends again.
Use both hands to pick up the chair.
See how easily it comes up!

You can lift things better
when you use both your hands.
A magnet, too, works better when
the two ends are close and work
together to pick up things that have
iron in them.
Straight magnets!
Curved magnets!

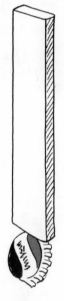

Both kinds have strong ends!
The ends can pick up things
that have iron in them.
But—
both ends working together can
pick up *heavier* things that have
iron in them.
When you are not using your curved magnet,
put an iron nail across both ends of the magnet.
This will keep your magnet strong for a long
time.

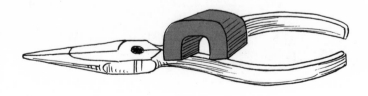

HOW CAN MAGNETS BE USED TO HELP YOU FIND DIRECTION?

A magnet can point out direction.
Do you want to see how?
Tie one end of a thin string around
the middle of the magnet.
Walk to the middle of the room.
Hold the loose end of the string
and let the magnet hang freely in the air.
Soon the magnet will stop turning.

Ask an adult to tell you which side
of the room is the north side.

One end of your magnet will point
toward that side of the room.

Print the letter N on that end of the
magnet pointing toward the north.

Now you can find "north" wherever
you are.

You can find north in the street.

You can find north in the park.

You can find north in a boat.

All you have to do is to let this magnet
hang freely at the end of a string and
wait until it stops turning.

The end that you marked with an N
will always point toward the north.

You can also use your magnet
to help you find the other directions—south,
east, and west.

Fasten the other end of the string on
your magnet to a table top.   Let the magnet
hang close to the floor.

Now draw a large circle on a sheet
of paper.

Write the letters of the four directions
this way on your paper:

$$\begin{array}{c} \text{N} \\ \text{W} \!-\!\!\!+\!\!\!-\! \text{E} \\ \text{S} \end{array}$$

Place the paper on the floor under
the magnet.

You know that when the magnet
stops turning, one end will point toward
the north.

Turn the paper so that the letter N
is under that magnet end which points north.

You have made your own compass!

Now you can find the other directions—
south, east, and west.

Look at your paper.

The letter S shows you where south is.

The letter E shows you where east is.

The letter W shows you where west is.

You have read your own compass!

WHAT IS THE RIGHT WAY TO USE A COMPASS THAT YOU BUY IN A STORE?

The compass you buy in a store does not look like the compass you made.

But it works exactly as yours does.

It is a small box with a small magnet pointer which turns around inside the box.

The directions north, south, east, and west are printed under the magnet pointer.

This compass is used just as yours was used to find directions.

The darker or the pointed end of the magnet pointer *always* points north.

To find north with this compass, you turn the box until the letter N is under the end of the magnet pointer that points north.

You can also find east, south, and west
just as you did with your homemade compass.

You can use this compass to find
direction wherever you may be—in the house,
in the street, in the park, in a boat.

Be sure to keep the compass away
from anything that has iron in it because the
magnet pointer in the compass would
turn toward the iron. This would keep the
compass from working correctly.

Do you know who uses this
kind of compass?

Boy Scouts use it.

Captains of ships use it.

Pilots of airplanes use it.
Explorers use it.

Compasses help many people
find direction on the land, on the seas,
and in the air.

HOW CAN YOU MAKE YOUR OWN MAGNET?

You have had fun making a homemade compass.

Now you can have fun making your own magnet.

It is very easy to make one!

All you need is a steel darning needle and a magnet. You can use a steel needle because steel is made from iron.

Rub the needle many times on one end of your magnet, moving the needle in the same direction each time.

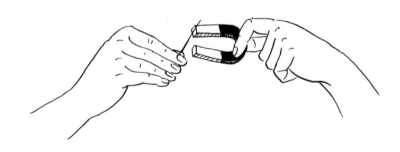

And then—
touch the needle to a paper clip.
The clip sticks to the needle!
You have made your own magnet!
This needle-magnet works the same
way as any other magnet.

You can use this needle-magnet to
pick up small things made of iron or steel.

You can use this magnet as
the magnet pointer of your homemade
compass.

HOW CAN YOU MAKE AN ON-AND-OFF MAGNET?

When you rubbed the darning needle with your magnet, you made a magnet that will work for a long time.

Would you like to know how to make a magnet that works only when you want it to work?

You need a long iron nail, a long piece of thin, covered, bell wire, a few clips, and a dry cell. The dry cell is used to make electricity.

Wind the wire around the nail about twenty times.

Take off the covering of both ends of the wire.

Connect *one* bare end of the wire to *one* screw on top of the dry cell.

Try to pick up the clips with one end
of the nail.

Do not be unhappy if the nail does
not pick up the clips.

You have not yet made your on-and-off
magnet.

But—

connect the *other* end of the wire to the *second*
screw on the top of the dry cell.

Leave the first end of the wire connected to
the first screw.

Now touch the nail to the clips.
Surprised?
The nail picks up the clips.
You have made a magnet!

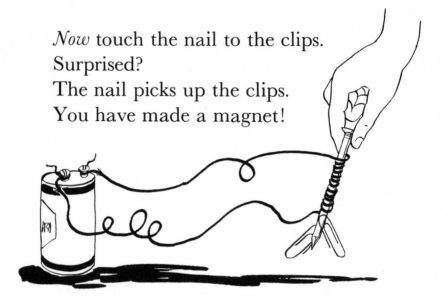

What do you think would happen to the
clips that were picked up by the nail if
you disconnected *one* end of the wire from
the dry cell?
Try it!
You will see that the clips will drop
to the table.
Why did the clips fall off the nail?
The nail has stopped being a magnet!
Put the wire back on the screw
and try to pick up the clips once more.
It works again!
The nail is a magnet again!

Take the wire off—the clips fall off!
The nail is not a magnet!
Can you guess why these things
happen each time?
As long as both ends of the wire
are connected to the dry-cell screws,
the electricity keeps going through the wire
that is wound around the nail.

This is what makes the nail become
a magnet.

As soon as the wire is disconnected,
the electricity stops going through the wire.
The nail stops being a magnet.

You have made a magnet that
is a magnet only when you want it
to be one.

You have made an on-and-off magnet.

We call this an electromagnet because
it uses electricity.

You can have fun playing
with your electromagnet when
you pick up and drop things that have
iron in them.

HOW CAN AN ELECTROMAGNET PICK UP AND DROP A HEAVY LOAD?

People who work in scrap-iron yards make work easier and safer for themselves by using a very large electromagnet.

They make their electromagnet from a large iron plate instead of a nail.

They use heavy covered wire instead of thin covered wire.

They use a great deal of electricity instead of the little electricity of a dry cell.

When the workers are ready to pick up heavy pieces of iron, they move the plate onto the pieces and turn on the electricity.
The electricity goes through the wire.
The iron plate becomes a magnet!

The magnet picks up the heavy
iron pieces.

When the workers are ready to put
the iron pieces into a truck, they move
the plate, which holds the iron pieces,
so that it is over the truck.

Then they turn off the electricity.

The electricity stops going through the wire.

The iron plate is not a magnet!

The iron pieces drop into the truck!

They have made a magnet that is
a magnet only when they want it to be.

They have made their electromagnet
work for them.

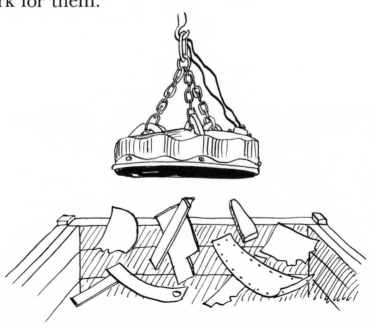

WHERE DO ELECTROMAGNETS WORK IN YOUR HOME?

Electromagnets work in your home
when you push buttons to ring doorbells

when you turn on the television set
when mother uses the vacuum cleaner
or the washing machine
and
when you run your electric train!

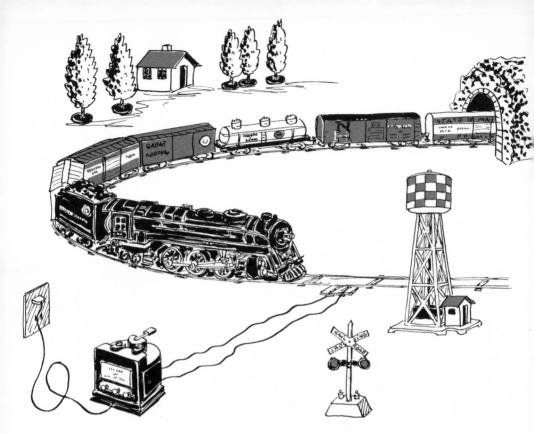

You do not see the electromagnets
because they are hidden in the bells, in
the machines, and in your engine.

But—

they are at work when the electricity
goes through the wires around the
electromagnets.

Electromagnets help to make work easier.

Electromagnets help to bring enjoyment
to everyone.

Long magnets
Short magnets
Fat magnets
Thin magnets

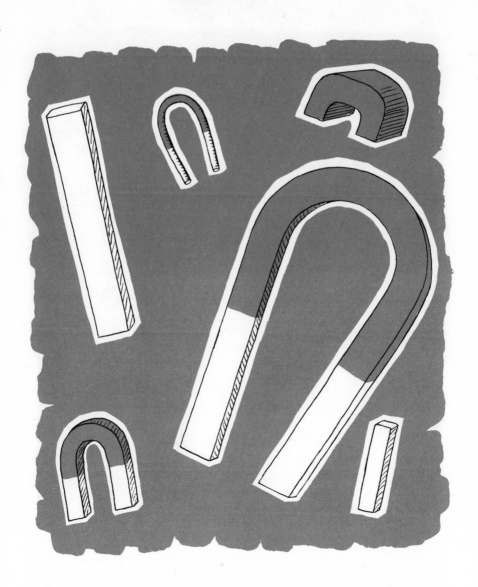

Where does the word "magnet" come from?

There is a story of long, long ago about a boy whose name was Magnes.

This boy, who lived in a country far, far away, helped his father take care of their sheep.

Every boy who took care of sheep in those days carried a wooden rod with an iron tip. So did Magnes.

One day, as Magnes was walking along watching the sheep and using the rod as a cane, he suddenly felt the rod stick to a large rock in the ground.

He was surprised!
He wondered why it had happened.
He told his father about it.
His father told all the neighbors.
Everybody wondered about this
wonderful stone!

This stone, which became known as "lodestone," is really a magnet-stone, and iron sticks to it.

Perhaps the word "magnet" comes from the name of this shepherd boy, Magnes.

No

      one

         really

            knows!

ABOUT THE AUTHORS AND ARTIST

Tillie S. Pine has been engaged in teaching and teacher education for many years. She has taught in the New York City school system, and for the last ten years has been on the staff of the Bank Street College Workshop in its experimental program of teacher education. She has lectured to teacher, parent, and student groups in New York and nearby cities, and with Workshop colleagues has collaborated in much "teacher help" material. Mrs. Pine is a resident of New York City and Westport, Connecticut, and is married to Nathan S. Pine of Dauber and Pine Bookshop, New York City.

Joseph Levine is principal of Public School 48, Bronx, New York, and has been a science teacher in the New York City school system for a great number of years. In addition to their book collaboration, Mr. Levine and Mrs. Pine have written a number of elementary science bulletins which are used throughout the city school system. Mr. Levine lives with his wife and three children in Flushing, Long Island, New York.

Anne Marie Jauss has illustrated over 25 books, including Newell's *Space Book for Young People,* and has written and illustrated *The River's Journey* and *Discovering Nature the Year Round.* She was born in Munich and studied at the State Art School there. In 1932 she left Germany and lived in Lisbon until 1946, when she came to the United States, and is now an American citizen. She has had a number of exhibits in New York City, and some of her drypoints are in the Print Collection of the New York Public Library. Miss Jauss makes her home in New York City.